Sleepwalker's Songs
New & Selected Poems

by
James Cervantes

Sleepwalker's Songs: New & Selected Poems
Copyright 2012 by James Cervantes

Cover photo and design by James Cervantes

Cervantes, James.
 Sleepwalker's songs : new & selected poems / by James Cervantes.
     p. cm.
 ISBN 978-0-9836668-1-3 (alk. paper)
 I. Title.
 PS3553.E78S54 2012
 811'.54--dc23
                               2012010901

H\s
HAMILTON STONE EDITIONS

Acknowledgments

I am grateful to the editors of the following journals and magazines for permission to reprint poems first published therein:

"A Case for My Life," On Barcelona, http://onbarcelona.blogspot.com/, 2012
"Lament," "Puffball Acceptance," "Ology," Otoliths, November, 2011
"Seasonal" & "Demise," Truck, October 2011, ed. Kelly Cherry
"Gladdy's Blues," "Fountain," "Update,"Hinchas de Poesia, #4
http://www.hinchasdepoesia.com/Hinchas/HINCHAS_FOUR/cervantes.html
"Shock Value," SOL: English Writing in Mexico, March, 2011,
http://www.solliterarymagazine.com/poetry/jim-cervantes-shock-value/
"Cone of Uncertainty," Tata Nacho #1, September, 2008,
http://tatanacho.wordpress.com/
"Third Hand Tale: West Virginia," Linebreak #38, October, 2008
http://linebreak.org/72/third-hand-tale-west-virginia/
"Number Three of Photo Album Shuffled," Big Bridge, Vol. 3, No. 3
http://www.bigbridge.org/BB14/WAR09.HTM#JCervantes
"Poems That Arrived Without a Briefcase," "Two Visionary Stories,"
"Idyll Beneath a Thunderhead," Merge, Fall 2007
"Magnetic Express" appeared in Tattoo Highway #7

Other poems are from the following collections:

from Mr. Bondo's Unshared Life, Vida Loca Books, 2007.
Temporary Meaning, Hamilton Stone Editions, 2006.
Changing the Subject, in collaboration with Halvard Johnson, Red Hen Press, March, 2004.
Live Music, chapbook, Pecan Grove Press, August, 2001.
The Headlong Future, New Rivers Press, St. Paul, MN, 1990.
The Year Is Approaching Snow, W.D. Hoffstadt & Sons, Syracuse, NY, 1981.

Contents

Here & There

Alternate Table of Contents

from *The Year Is Approaching Snow*

Sleepwalker's Songs
New & Selected Poems

A Life

This Junction

There's not a cloud in the jar,
not a drop of rain in the drawer.
The beach falls out of my shoe
and my little finger picks a gull
out of my ear. I wipe trees
from my glasses
and slowly fly to work,
fuel the wheels, climb
a tunnel that's gone to seed
and left bullet holes in the sky.
Phone calls seem to know each other.
I let them talk while I listen
to the town on my wall,
where E. Santa Fe wraps
its arms around N. Leroux,
flicks a cigarette into the gutter.

Gulf Coast Blues

The boy kicks gravel in his drive
and up pops a scallop shell. Grave

shadows of cumulus turn it gray,
but in the sun, country-western,

gospel, and violin love music
mix like rusty wire and vanish

like a fuse of laden air.
You can almost see a fish drying,

a woman's leg drying, the smoke
from a stack and from a barbeque.

Saturday morning's first beers
sweat in all those right hands

while the left ones power-steer.
You do see the woman's bare leg

and foot stuck out the window,
so still, and the dune grass

bending over, turning silver,
like some new revolving world.

Out of Fever

The dogs do not move today
and the tallest trees are limp.
There's a white film on the broad leaves
of the cottonwood that a boy
wipes with one finger. His sister
has a fever and will not rise today.

He notices other clear
green streaks and thinks that maybe
these are his sister's, and runs
to the faucet. His brow has become wet
and he washes that too.

Only the screen doors are closed.
He looks in. His mother
is strangely blurred by the screen
but the cloth she carries
is luminous and drops large
slow drops. For two days

the boy spends his time like this,
like the clouds that are just
out there. He will not enter the room
where snakes startle his sister
and there are so many days and nights
in a short time. His sister
looks new when she wakes.

Roosters and Train Whistles

Somehow, they've always been there
in the dark when I wake up
anywhere, despite absence of track,
though most naturally in the island city
in Iowa's ocean of farmland; Flagstaff,
where tracks parallel the main drag
and thin air dampens flutter and cluck;
in childhood, where they were like right
and left hands clapping me awake,
uncle's chickens and the Southern Pacific
crowing together; Brattleboro,
where roosters woke as the whistle neared
and I knew I'd make the station on time.
And now, two blocks from the Hudson River,
the hoot of a freight cuts like a French horn
through traffic's tremolo and a rooster
struts from the dark into its missing voice.

Third Hand Tale: West Virginia

This from those who drove out
to see the others drive their cars
around the church, up and down
the road in front, the one out back,
back and forth the roads on the sides
until worship ended and the girls came out
sweaty from hallelujahs. Each driver
beckoned one into a car and drove her out
not too far where the woods thickened
and they could park so that no car
was within sight of another. Then sound
took over and what they said they heard
was birthing and the spirit spilling forth.

Last Stops

One of the clergy grandfathers
would take me on a rural route, a green,
streamlined bus with a restroom stop
on the way to his church, which was stale
from being closed up all week.

It was a two bus trip to Mary Nell's,
but sometimes I'd skip the transfer
just to walk and smell the neighborhood of soaps,
and I swear I could smell the brick.

My stop on the Hardy Street line
was bare earth parking lot, with a yard
of railroad ties across the street, and a store
behind me, where I'd duck in to look
at the owner's daughter, who vanished
into a New York modeling career.

I'd wave to people I knew on the porches
between the first two stops on the way downtown,
dizzy myself with a motionless stare
as we accelerated past factories, a mixture
of hot metal and burned coffee filling the bus.

I loved the swoosh of air brakes and the doors
folding in like wings, the dash onto the sidewalk
as if I had a purpose, and the sighs of a revolving door,
injecting perfume and leather into the diesel air.

Signal Deaths

1. for Victor Power

The crow in a graveyard
looks up at me like an old man
charged with the census
of his village,
but iridescent blackness
goes back to hunting
in the grass of the dead.

I wouldn't have noticed it
but for my friends,
who, on the day of Victor's death,
claimed to see or speak
with doubles of their long dead friends.

Nor would I have stayed
to become the crow's business
if its pecking in the grass
had not reminded me
of those who turn their backs
and never face us again,

or those who note our drinking
but never hear the toast.

2. Vera

Print, print: the sound of a file
that diminishes nothing. Yesterday,

time fell back. It is darker
when I wake up. Too often,

I see the heron turn whiter
as it rises from the bayou
beside the funeral home.
She may have died
a few days before, this aunt of mine,
but here she is, her face
supplanting each face
in the viewing room, coming round
until I too accept it.

It was after that the heron rose,
unnoticed at first,
then yawing above willow
and cottonwood, going away
above the odd neighborhood,
a few homes
and the gray docks
that ship and receive.

3. Mr. & Mrs. Death

Mr. & Mrs. Death, driving an MG
hit the tall, lanky fellow
I am helping across the street.
Upon which Mr. Death vaults
from the sporty weapon, though I don't realize
it's Mr. Death until I look at his lady,
who is beyond doubt Mrs. Death,
paler than albino, with the grin
of a dog that grins.

This could have been
El Dio De Los Muertes , except
I saw myself from within myself.
It was my usual body asleep

up to the skillful transition
at the neck, where, quite bone-like,
I held my skull. Ruthless equations,
rattling bone planks, this unfaithful bridge!

The Fires in Oil Drums

In winter, the fires in oil drums
are like the crone's voice
repeating a child's complaint.

In our search for a likeness
we have come to these endless stoops
where men and women are hunched

over the red domes, fallen
like the stone finials behind them.
We see her features

Scattered among faces—brother, cousin,
the child—but our hope
is the white parabola above each fire,

where there is no threshold
for warmth, just ice
in the lungs, as when one

turns from the drum for the door.
Now smoke complicates dusk
in the east, and evening

is a café on the dog-leg
of a twisted summer, under
its close roof

the nakedness that drinks
an after-image of fire.

The Following Is True if the Poincare Conjecture Is True

I

*In topology, a coffee cup is equivalent to a doughnut because one can be
continuously deformed into the other, with the cup's handle becoming the
doughnut's hole. But both are different from a sphere because no amount of
stretching creates or removes a hole.*

It's December and I sit in the office
trying unsuccessfully to begin the series
based on topology and attempts to prove
the Poincare conjecture. I realize
in staring at the calendar
that it's been five years
since I last spoke with you in person.
The same goes for James A., who writes long,
single-spaced, unparagraphed letters
about $99 airfares from NYC to Belgium,
or Jody, who writes from St. Ives,
tells me who's been there, and includes
the fishing report, and Greg's Christmas letter
is about a translation project in Portland,
and comes with Volume 4, Number 1,
of a magazine I've never seen, but which he says
we spawned somehow. I can't figure out
what he's talking about. It simply looks
familiar, like another strand of memory,
as if he's presented one space more
than the three I can visualize. Or, I've imagined
one of you sitting here in the cane chair,
lifting a cup from the polished burl, and you
have imagined me sitting in whatever chair,
lifting from a table what I must.

II

The 80-year struggle to settle the Poincare conjecture testifies to the fantastic
complexity that arises in exploring spaces of more than the three we can visualize.
It has also shown again and again that whole realms of mathematics can be
opened up by attempts to prove the obvious.

No matter what the ruler
laid on the map says,
they are all equally distant. It is the same
from the desert to the granite
underpinnings of Brooklyn, from this
volcanic rim to the other, from the fishing grounds
off St. Ives back to the desert.

One smells the natural abundance
of azaleas and rhododendrons,
another the predominant tang of evergreens,
another orange blossoms and jacaranda, foxglove
and hawthorn for another, and for one
a bitter geranium that bends to no wind
this side of a sooty window.

They wake to the ocean
shoving rocks around, the conversation
between wind and mild rain,
the quiet of a desert whose sounds
are small and hidden, and the street's
amplification of motors.

Nonetheless, one day the light
is nearly the same everywhere.
The effect is to make the distance
from windows to the ordinary sights
exactly what it should be, equal
to the stone wall from here, or to the naked
winter elm with its loaded branch.

III

. . . features such as curvature or holes are only apparent from an outside vantage point in the third dimension. An observer confined to the surface just sees two dimensions, [which raises] a problem: How can he tell what kind of shape his surface is taking?

Camellias bloom
around the little *cul-de-sac,*
as if the neighbors had agreed
some years ago. I see no others

until the short-cut,
where they bloom in deeper,
darker yards, and the air
along the street is cool

I could drive on
but turn where I work, where camellias
once again appear, though whiter
and ganged up like clouds. They sway

and send perfume somewhere.
The breeze that moves them
might reach you tomorrow. It may
ripple up the slopes

through aspen groves, appear to
rest, then return as the room
that seems suddenly cleared.

IV

. . . physicists in the post-Einstein era, trying to understand the structure of spacetime have realized that space can be curved in higher dimensions — impossible to visualize, and not easy to calculate with, either.

We live
with one page of the calendar
and an hour
is a coupling of voices,
much like the random lighting
of lamps below a plane:

seeing them
links them, and the darkness
with them as well.

How does one arrive
here so happy? If you take
the little round lights
and turn them, they are the same.

They have no flat places
so you might set them down.
This is why
people look at us, you there, me here.

We carry the same thing
and it is all we can do to explain.

V

The final part of the early papers [Rourke's] – with the most crucial logic –
seemed most vague. "I don't know how to answer that," Rourke said. "I had the
feeling when I was writing it that I was putting the same amount of detail
everywhere. Anyway, I think now it's just a question of letting it sink into
people's subconscious -- More and more of it will sink in, until it's obvious."

The whole thing is somewhat easier now,
addressing you, and not talking to the idea.

This morning the day arrived
like a pale yellow plate
over the industrial end of town,
and the cold smell of leaves
slipped over the transom.

It was all that was required
to cause a break, to have me observe
that the digital clock and courthouse chimes
didn't match, and that it was time to begin.

The "Perspectives" section
of the paper almost cancelled
the Poincare conjecture --
something about "Radiation
Equivalent Man."

It was another idea, like a shelf of smoke
above a little town, tucked in and battling winter.

VI

"We're living in a three-dimensional world and we don't know what it is because we've never been to infinity," Rourke said. "There's no reason to think of sitting inside of something. You have to think in terms of what it is, in itself."

It is like leaving toys
in the little yellow house,
built for a mother-in-law
and now rented in six-month spells.

It is barely visible from uphill,
like a dime-store amethyst
suspended in a green nap,
nestled in the grid
of gray and buff streets,
with the model railroad
going, cutting almost center
in the town growing up.

It is of growing up
that we speak, gaining conviction
from the aerial view. This spring
is the one of blackened tulips,
limbs cracking under snow.
Will you take
another six-month lease,
or sit longer on this hill?

This summer
is the one of fires held back,
the one of spontaneous roses.

* *All epigraphs are taken from an article by James Gleick which appeared in the October 12, 1986 edition of* The New York Times.

A Persona: *Nine Poems from Mr. Bondo's Unshared Life*

*

The unresolved music of wind chimes
persists in the afternoon,
always after the wind has passed
and without a beginning.

Be gone, stay, begin now,
wing, be gone, he hears them chime.
They stop before the pine says *hush*,
then they follow with *gone, now stay*.

Gone where, stay where, begin what?
He cannot ask because *wing* chimes,
then *now* and *stay*. He is gone
before the pine is still, a wing now,

without a beginning, without a way.

*

At eight or ten he came to know himself
sitting on a window ledge, lost in the envelope
of a panorama, then a tunnel
in the air to the coast.

"Boy!" his mother yelled, and Mr. Bondo
lost his balance, grunting
like an animal phrasing a question.

Later, when window and view were one,
he'd forget the window seat
upon which he sat, and that he was looking
through the bay window, over the rooftops
at cypress leaning from the sea.

These days, he sometimes
holds a window, steps through it
and forgets it
because he knows the way back.

He was that way with a person once.
She lives over there, like a view
from her window, and Mr. Bondo waves.

*

The Law of Remarkable Resemblance
was born this good day when Mr. Bondo decided
the world does not run on wires, or waves, or particles.
It runs, instead, on chains of tiny mirrors
that face each other like half-opened wings.
Excited resemblance finds itself
over and over in the face of each mirror
and spreads the word to its reflections.
They might, Bondo mused, be influenced
by an observer, so he looks over the shoulder
of a resemblance and is instantly included.

*

When Mr. Bondo awoke with his hair on fire,
he did the only thing he could do.

Having hung his drenched pajamas on a line,
he returned to find his bed unscathed,

no sign of frayed wires, no smoldering butts,
no ozone from a possible visitation.

Bondo meditated beneath his frizzy hair
until he was lost in the cobalt blue

of a mountain photo taken years ago, a puff
of white cloud to the right and above the peak

in late afternoon, when he'd forgotten the hours
following skittery paths, speaking out loud

to bushy Kaibab squirrels, so frank and open
with their stares. He remembered the hour

and how the sun would be setting if he didn't
begin his descent. Quickly now,

and never mind the slipping.

*

Night after night, he digs deeply
in his yard for the golden helmet
buried somewhere near the base
of a monolithic boulder. Coronado
chose well, as the earth is soft
and there are no rocks save the giant one.

The summer nights wear the map down
to wet tissue, and Bonco is apprehensive
until he realizes he's dug the "X" so deep
he'll never lose his way. Three angels,
predictable in white chiffon and footless,
flutter their robes to cool his brow.

Surprised at the ease with which the earth
gives way, he places the first of three lilies
but cannot remove his hand from the pale
timekeeper, this harbinger revealed
by a peeling golden sheath, its roots
like hair buried more dead than alive.

*

Summer settles in like a heavy guest
leaving too large an impression
in his favorite chair. It extends
beyond his arbitrary home
into a mountain retreat, where a man
fails to brush a leaf from his lover's hair
and Bondo shrugs as if he were that man
and the woman was forgotten for the leaf.

He looks at the trees along the street –
mountain ash no taller than one storey –
and senses a fullness without any sign
of opening leaves. The sky cannot carry
any more light and the mountains
cannot snag clouds. He will go now,
but return looking for that edge
when the town looks cut from air.

*

Mr. Bondo is two people in the world
this afternoon on the viney campus
and two people again at the grocery store.
He is maybe one person in the dog's
deep brown eyes, and nothing
to the desert milkweed
whose meager thirst he satisfies.

He thinks there might have been three
of him for his wife, possibly four
when he would leave for walks alone.
Absent one. zero on a keyboard,
untouched while fingers take
one order of letters into another.

In this mood, his friends multiply
into unknowns. One turns a smile
toward him and into his eyes
and he knows; one of several backs
walking away and he knows. But who
is that in a story in Chicago, driving

past what he thought was her hometown,
ignoring signs held out to her, running
right through a cloud of details? Mr. Bondo
thinks of a crowd on a ship waving
to a waving crowd on shore, and how
easily he could be in both.

*

Does everyone wonder about the birds
that come and go in the yard? Are those really
the same two doves every morning, the same grackles
arriving like a gang on vacation, the very same
hummingbird going eye-to-eye with a pair
of perfect, odorless blossoms that blink?

Or do they all strut, squawk, and stare
in the same way on any stage? He wonders
because he wishes a special usefulness
for himself and his yard: that he has planted
the right things for delight and sustenance
of birds, that his cats swoon and are paralyzed
by so much bounty, that his dog

merely cocks its head like Mr. Bondo
when a hummingbird hovers before him,
mesmerizing with its blur of wings, the black dwarves
of its eyes blinding him to the color of air that surrounds it.

This evening, Mr. Bondo makes stew,
a *boeuf bourguignonne* with good burgundy
because it complements the smell of dead leaves,
those falling as they die, letting sunshine
hit the house from the east in November.

He will have to rake, but thinks he will wait
until the trees are bare, until *the sun's*
critical angle is significant and marked
transition occurs. He read of this
somewhere and will apply it to his life.

His neighbor is playing music outdoors,
tacking lights to his eaves. Smell of manure
for winter rye lingers, so Bondo goes inside
for the onion, bay leaf, thyme, the soupy mix
of tomato, oils, and beef. He sniffs and decides

there will be no tree this year, no fussing
with lights or the history of ornaments.
Fainter smells of carrot and mushroom
follow him around the house, piquant
green pepper, perhaps the water and salt.

A Case for My Life

1. Whereas James is physically continuous with Jimmy
(inclusive of, but not dependent upon baby footprint)

2. and whereas Jimmy was declared most likely dead
(James hovering above white-clad Jimmy in hospital bed)

3. and inasmuch certain memory connections between
Jimmy and James were lost in a chronic naiveté

4. (thirty different names for thirty women
in addition to two that stood out, four forgotten)

5. and in consideration of witness statement
(Pamela) that "You don't know who you are."

6. and further consideration of the detritus
of a dozen years (curator unknown)

7. hash-marked and herein named as bad debt
repossession, abandonment, and various

8. arrangements and partnerships classified here
as "severed," but not limited to such

9. in acknowledgement of "the butterfly effect"
and in continuation of a life hereafter referred to

10. as "James," first-born of the first-born "Jimmy"
latter name having currency among, but not limited to

11. individuals of the same genetic lineage, individuals
related through marriage, acquaintances claiming intimacy

12. and others listed in Schedule A, and pertaining
to the 25,892 days of "Jimmy"/James existence

13. affected by this claim, with the understanding
that any future days are also subject to the claim

14. regardless of geographical place, such as
City-of-non-indigenous-palms, or Marketville

15. ghostly Jimmy and substantive James submit
the opinion that hazy identity formation

16. is no more a criminal act than nibbling the toes
of one's sweetheart, and do hereby enter a request

17. that cup of seawater known as "James" be poured
back into the sea, no longer distinguishable from it

18. from a day to be determined and thereafter.

The Dream World

A Place That Is the Same Elsewhere

I don't know what this has to do
with another unfinished thing,
but I saw in a dream the last
of a series of homes. It came
stripped of 200 years of history,
a red dusty road going to the end
of its course as it does in real life;
its banks, because it seemed a dry bed,
were contoured as they are now, peopled,
built upon, littered with the future.
I traveled with a shadow-person, as is
often the case in dreams, playing cars
with real cars which shouldn't have been there,
but which he, fleshed now as a stranger,
wanted to move from atop a bank
into the dusty road with the strength
and expediency of dreams.

In the switching yard of dreams,
I accepted this research as a magnesium flare
shadow-person did not see. I had
the road to myself now, followed it,
ate up history, and came to the houses
that were as they are now: endangered,
but also blessed by a window. In time,
among the jokes, the deaths, and affairs
of those who live there, I will say,
because I am caught with them,
I had a dream about this place.

Garden of Antiquities

Here is the road that has always run on only one side of the woods. On the right, the east, are the woods, and on the left is the caretaker's house. The caretaker is asleep in his boat on the pond just inside the woods. He is visible from just about any spot on the road.

From the boat, looking west, the fields are endless. There is a slight rise toward infinity, but since the whole horizon does this, the imagined dip to the pond becomes physical.

A dotted line across the average middle of the pond would reveal a slice of darkness to the east. It is toward that darkness that a man walks purposefully, having stopped at the caretaker's house for directions, and who now unbelievably misses the caretaker on the pond.

He stops at a hut, enters, and sees a crude shelf on which there is a doll with half-closed eyes and crazed porcelain flesh, though its body feels like a stuffed bird. He dusts it off and takes it with him, continuing his walk until he comes to a road that has always run on only one side of the woods.

How Dreams Resolve

I am holding the hand of a hideously androgynous
man and woman who will not make up his or her mind
and return to being the brown-haired woman on the escalator
who turned and touched my shoulder one second longer
than a stranger should, transmitting to me on the gliding
upward moving stairs the push, resistance, warmth and
acceptance of her naked body, though she was stylishly dressed
in a brown tweed suit the living color of her hair, a dark tone
against which her paleness flashed at the very moment
her braids untwined, floating us off the escalator mid-floor
onto the dirt of our nest with a pleasant thump, her buttocks
and thighs picking up the grit but with no objection from me.

Idyll Beneath a Thunderhead

We named her Fiesta Galana, after the two towns in which we'd met.
There was a flounder in a sandal, gasping next to little brown toes.

Her arms, shoulders, and thighs were equally bronzed: a fractal resonance.
The abandoned bed, a sepia version, was jammed in a sky-blue corner.

We'd get the droozers, dark bubbles inviting us through the open door.
Forensic documentaries were thunderstorms on a once blue screen.

In the shack with a satellite dish, the lampshade danced to the wind.
Dry fronds crackled. When we consulted our watches it was time to go.

Want Rant

You foolishly blurt out something
unattainable. It has the ring

of fantasy, wishful thinking, plain bullshit,
and you want the conversation to quit.

Whispers to a thirty-year-old
of soul vespers from a fifty-year-old

soul which is actually younger.
There is real physical hunger

for food, nothing else. But that
is also metaphysical squat

from an observer who craves
something in-between, who caves

in to the mirror, as if his face
is out of place and possibly scarce

where it belongs. And you know
this is when ill winds blow,

when exoskeletons bow,
smooth faces wanting it now.

Number Three of Photo Album Shuffled

It has *chinzwa ookoo* parking lot or parade
aftermath
punk-stick in jello maybe

flighty smell of a new shirt artfully ripped
between third and fourth column
inside window to elbow's achievement
of lizard skin

single ping of windchime
in the desert
come upon a rotting corpse

see sweet sweet
poor genitalia so close to thorns

so crumple dishonesty
into the plastic bag hanging
simply the result of tiredness

third grade classroom derangement
iris effect not Ken Burns

a grade is a magic marker
synesthetic concerto for
            two pianos
            attack trumpet
            four little hammers on a pipe
standing room only in the inner ear

oomphee solos
a light touch upon a stranger's shoulder
(wince) *(move for the clown dammit,*

enter world
we have hit no one lately how about you?

Ology

A new style does not necessarily recapitulate an older one, but it's interesting in costume: In back, begin at the nape of the neck with a daring mix of feathery reds and purples, becoming more profuse at mid-spine, then a progression of new chords at the coccyx in luminescent greens and blues that trail a bit on the floor. The front: black sleeves from armpit to wrist, black leg-wraps from groin to ankle, an attenuated rich plum vest whose top is just below the breastbone (male or female), is unbuttoned (no buttons anyway), and spreads so that about four inches of abdomen are visible down to the pelvic bone where the inverted V of the vest focuses the eye inevitably on the V of the genital area, where pubic hair is shaved and replaced by a clutch of delicate ribbons that provide glimpses of genitalia (male or female), overtly and covertly. The ribbons, however, are not a lubricant.

On Sleeping in a Strange Bed

You carry your head in parchment
to the specialist.
You win a sweepstakes
and swim in the neon blue
of webpages, dabble in water
and plumes of metallic confetti.

You toot a horn and light a fuse.
Girls spray from the white-hot dervish,
women gather around you.
What heaven is that you turn from,
sweaty-backed hulk, to turn
to another, full of orchids, full of fish?

Though asleep, your head itches
on an unfamiliar pillow. You drool
like the idiot marrying a wooden horse,
twitch as your eyes beneath their lids
go back and forth from desert to ocean,
ocean to desert, freshly turned earth
between them. Tendrils poke upward and curl.

Your head has been severed again
and you discuss this with interest
with another headless soul. *Oh what will we do?*
But, more interestingly, why? The solution
is to wake and walk to the bathroom
through coffee's scented hook, embarrassed
by *Good morning* and a slackening penis.

Lament

Rococo is mentioned at the same time *ornate* is mentioned.
The customizer is a customer for mass customization.
One doesn't ask why a neighbor looks stricken and throws
    a suitcase into her car.
A November moment when people side-step into the sun
    from shade gone bitter
and recall July when they side-stepped into the shade.
There is a kind of hurrying-back. One seeks elucidation
and has recourse to television. Breaking news might explain,
or an interrupted game. Still at the same party
where three women here and two men over there
speak at the same time, you feel deflated in your clothes.
There is always distraction. The show called "Tourist Planet"
is remembered by looking out the window just to see.
Or an old man addresses his johnson:
"You can get rid of wrinkles. So? Big deal.

The Old Man Dreams

Two bodies lie by a pond that has two shores: one that seems casual, with roots, twigs, and leaves that slip under the surface; the other formal, its fine gravel raked in sinuous lines, the terminus of a narrow road. The bodies are of two kinds --wood and flesh-- and they lie on the casual shore staring at the forest umbrella. A carriage comes by the road, stops, and two men step down. They crush around the pond and arrive at the bodies. The first man pulls a handmirror from his vest and holds it before the fleshy nostrils. The second man simply lifts the dummy by its hinged arms and legs, but stops momentarily while the first man breezily passes the mirror before the wooden nostrils. The dummy is propped in the corner of a seat, then both men slowly and clumsily haul the heavier body, laying it on the floor between the seats. The ride is bumpy. The ventriloquist does not move, but the dummy time and again drops its jaw, rolls its eyes, and bangs the seat with its heels.

Seven Incarnations

1.

Tune your ear to other, for your eyes are two lamps at sea. Likening is dead, or so it was told on a small, dry shore. The sun shone through brown Mathilda's threadbare dress, a broad Gaelic hand clasping her bare left foot, the other flailing while sea-spray flew from her brow. Sonniksenn dropped sail before this came to pass, creased that self-same shore when water lapped its trees. The rest he made up as he was wont to do, and there it was on dimpled paper, as real as real can be. There were clothes, too, that looked shat upon, and rags of skin draped on timbers that washed ashore. Those who landed shuddered as the sea went out, and one said the wind told tales when it blew into his ear. "Put it on dimpled paper," it said, "Use the blood-red seal."

2.

At the end of a long, rude road, there is little salt to be licked from flesh. Those who are heavy and slow make their way by wit, or with packets of flags to which they owe no allegiance. Jackals chew on leather hinges and guano burns through vowels, so that one man's horde becomes another's scattered treasure. In the fifth month, constellations fade over the southern horizon and new ones rise in the north. It is then the tall man passes them on the ridges above, hunched over with heavy pack though still outpacing them. Something sparks in the sky and drifts slowly down: a yellow feather. Then, as if its shadow followed, a green feather settles not three steps after they have claimed the other. They are in a land where birds sing with flutes.

3.

Imago never took himself literally. After all, there he was, living with a woman who was his imagined wife, and who responded to him even when he was silent. His job was to dispose of bodies bloated with death and he had to keep moving from villages whose families he outlived. He'd long forgotten his imagined wife when he entered life as an astronomer, fixing from every position, and naming with every name the star that waxed and finally waned. Imago's star was a secret until he sailed away, landed, and followed the man who showed him a simple "x" scratched on a curving tower's stones, where two holes lined up to reveal nothing.

4.

She strokes his brow, gently holds him down when a twig snaps and he jerks upward. She strokes his brow but now his eyes stay open. He is a world away from her. A boar charges through the opening. Several heads poke through. The twig snaps twice, then three times. The dirt rises and coils inside. It/they make gore of her so easily, as if she has no bones. She strokes his brow and he rolls, rolls them over, enters her, bounces her on the earthen floor.

5.

In Orkney splash we springtime went, oofinit pass the cowee. Ach, bullpie! Hail, salade!

Harold's farm lay ruined, except for the barn which was cliff of stone. All about the flowers grew, those climbing ones that droop and tickle your arse between hay and stone.

Ten paces, leaning back as ye go, hair and heather combed by sea's steady wind. Way down there, stirred and clacking, scepters, broken wheels, bones in their hardiest clothes. The shattered boat needed a man. You know what we tossed. Hell yes! And soggy tomes for the sea's quick hunger.

6.

In a city of onions, smoke, and bells, tobacco, incense, and funeral pyres, bazouki and sitar, cymbals ringing, eddies of smoke and water, Giacomo fixes on the wrong woman. Tiny pearls bloom on her forehead and cheeks. She has countless hands he reaches for, misses, brushes, and claps, fingertips he fans -- then, for the blink of an eye, a wrist he holds between thumb and forefinger. Part of him speaks, part of him floats away. She smiles and crumbles, a crushed jewel.

It is a massive effort to quarter the body, sever the head, and remove heart and liver. For then seven lands must be found, or at least five separated by oceans and seas, the head to be left where his face is known. Finally, the liver is cast into an ocean and the heart buried on the rim of a cauldron. Vultures and jackals take the trunk where it lies scattered.

7.

Thus the sun followed me and was cause for the night-machine whose governor was none other, though operable by whoever dare approach. Deadly nightshade footnote: No way to compensate for eating the wrong grape; irretrieveable if entered with French finesse, shade on shade, the nether end of smoke. Bold strokes make the gears go. Morning mist burned off, a good shit, elbowing through mild sheep, stepping in/through whatever, living ten years past death. It is refreshingly optimal to have one foot in the nave and the other in a time when rain will come three days hence. Guaranteed, because the hint is in the tree frog's song, twined about the fern's unfurling.

The Proxy

The bulb swings and his melon shadow weighs on the first old man he's thrown to the floor. In the silence, while spectators stare through dust pounded from the planks, I hear what sounds like seeds sifting and settling in the defeated husk.

One, then another contestant takes him on, but it's the same as before: the shriveled bodies hurling themselves at each other, no striking with arms or legs, just the thud of trunk against leathery trunk. With his third victory, he makes the slightest acknowledgment of my presence, a mere turn that causes all the spectators to cheer me and begin slapping my back.

I am surprised and embarrassed by this pride that makes me look for him. My comforts call now like waves of heat, drawing me from the sulfurous room. He is gone, but again there is that sound as of a gourd lightly handled.

This Season

Et le printemps m'a apporte l'affreux rire de l'idiot
-Rimbaud, *A Season In Hell*

It was a romance with brick: each brick an island, a dome, reefs and archipelagos of porous brick, and between them the gray mortar, like low-slung clouds within the rise and fall of brick. Then, abruptly, like the crack of a frozen lake, the fluid yard found its boundaries.

Every doorway had its crazy niche, locked thighs that crumbled in spring's sweaty dew; every window its tableau, with full- bodied death crushing a maiden's breasts, his tongue driving into bone.

At last the trees obscure the street. The city is crazed with renovation. All night I hear jackhammers, sludge-pumps, the slap of lumber, trowels rasping. Stairways cover the old cliffs. One crisp morning the blue-print rises, dovecote within dovecote, beautiful graph through which the laughter rattles.

The Long Dream of a Life

Frost came but twice
and even the rains were scarce.
A patch of goldenrod
grew in the watery shadows
beneath his window. Letters,
reams of letters were carried
down the walk from the portico,
his tunnel through the ochre winter.

He scraped at his beard
and was shamed by the dry skin
that adhered to ink, that fell on the word "sorry."

To whom was he writing?
Someone distant, all distant,
his letters borne over the horizon.
Orion was closer. The garden
was as distant, the time from seed to harvest
the same as letter and answer.

"Sorry for the long delay. I
was busy. I was otherwise occupied.
The linden felt something today
and dropped some of its leaves."

The "I" and "thou."
Last night he dreamt the "I"
gone to the station to wish "thou" goodbye.
The station was bunker, a squared hole
from which the train would emerge.
He broke down and climbed
into someone's lap.

The temptation
was to give dream its lead,
let it decorate, lose "you" in "they."
He even waved. The window fogged
and the garden called him,
its watering, its shade
a whisper of mountain life.

It seemed flat, pressed
between thick sheets of cellophane,
only the grass at his feet
rising to inhabit the world.

*

Full, though not at flood,
the river lifted him,
brought him closer to the canopy
next to fulfilled banks. The dense hardwood
was not his symmetry and always seemed low,
as if to push one into a picnic.

Sprawled, he'd shared a passive feast,
lost nothing on the cleared ground
beneath a day-long shade, he and Pasqual
brimming with aspen, snowfield, and ptarmigan
while the two women rowed, trolling
at the edge of the sun-struck channel.

He tossed a rock into the livid green
and relished the sparks disturbed from its slowness.
A gust of wind turned the leaves, bleached the sky.
The ground rushed into the sudden calm, sealed them
in a vacuum with deadwood, leaves, the women's
scented clothes. But Pasqual and the women
spoke to him from outside.

He couldn't answer. His mouth was full of bark
from the stick that held his jaws apart.

*

A girl in crinoline
watched over him and he worked backward
to delve into the bundle
in her lap. Both of them
were photographed before a carpet
hung on the line; her hair, parted in the middle,
made the same dark pyramid as her skirts.
And beneath those skirts
her legs broke out in a shallow sweat,
teased by the knife-edged crinoline. In her care
the baby went bump. Sunlight crept across the yard,
releasing the dank smell of carpet.

*

The unseen orchestra played all night,
but as the sky is stripped at daybreak,
so the fundamentals
fell from his hearing. He heard
the secondary orchestra, the crystal gears,
wolf-tone engaged with harmonic. His arms,
the seen body, reached and grasped
while he slept, not wanting to wake
to that vast recessional.
So the night opened and curled,
revealing its silver spine.
he entered and dove
but did not feel, instead
was stained by darkness. Rising,
he struck a crystal pipe
that rang dully, then stumbled
and the whole night rang.

*

Dear Claire, a late summer & I must get out.
Anything but yellow air! A kettle
boiling in the kitchen, that's what I find
almost everywhere. Last night, when I got off the train,
the grass by the tracks was burning. The smoke
hung low around the station, but sort of boiled
at the tunnel. Little red lights
flickered here & there. Everyone
was busy & getting further away,
as if chasing something into a tunnel.
And then, Claire, there were two shots –
a nickel-plated revolver. I'd swear that gun
rose out of the tracks, or from the shiny wheels
that were now shrieking -- a glint taking shape.
But there was no one. Down by the tunnel
water hissed & steam rose quickly.
What was it, Claire? I walked home
annoyed by the crickets who knew nothing.
I know what you're thinking, but now I'll hallucinate
those fields before you & your Canadian air. The day
is gaining weight & I must leave you
for my blessed, though shallow, nap.

*

A Goodyear blimp sputtered across the sky.
There was a lie about the flash in Nevada.
Overhead, a year to the day
from one of those events, B-29's
flew in a V-formation. The pavement was hot
and the parade uncomfortable
even in khaki shorts. He burned his fingers
on the general's green convertible.

He wished for water
in that miasma of tar and oil.
He wished for the coolness of the slim blond in white.
On the long walk home,
he lay on the first lawn, used it up,
then ran into the plumber's supply
and drank long draughts from the fountain
in a maze of enameled steel, all white,
all with chromium stubs that drew gallons, columns
of transparent water, and he was filled with ice
whose needles begged exit from his flesh.

*

(two voices)

    He poled north,
stashed the pole and paddled through the narrows.
In this I see my life. Lunch in an eddy
nosed in, bow and stern in crevices.
     And in the eddies—
they splashed, imitating motion—*I see the possibilities*
seized honestly by the senses—the boat
knocked against the rocks—*the body,*
used in that realm, then put back
as what I see now.
  He rocked free, lost ground,
but paddles into a view of aspen. *Equivalents*
for what was forgotten, and what was forgotten—stunted spruce
now on a hillock with its skirt of shale—*as sweet*
as the possibilities
    that wave as I wave at them.
He slept in the boat he would leave,
    They are there too
dreamt the smooth round faces
    in elegant confusion with the seized
drifting over inches of clear water.

Words & Music

A Villanelle Returns From War

You have to make sense now.
Planes are in the air.
You have to speak up

before planes. You've bought all
there will be to buy. Say something
plain, make bye-bye. Tell everyone

you need this and this. What?
No flower in the kit?
In the kitchen, panes warm up,

whistle. See why there is no steam:
It's all fire and sand. It's pain
less flour, salt, and petals. Yell,

whistle, say some lower the living,
raise the dead, craft the air. Oh, and
bring people, take people. Ports

are drawers of the sea,
tables of land. Sit down, be sensible,
say something before you take off again.

Amaryllis

- after "Vignett: Amaryllis," a lithograph by Edvard Munch

Amaryllidaceae
is its family and belladonna
the one specie.
It's a lily, a tropical flower.
The ovary is congenitally joined
with the external envelope, a green star.

Amaryllis is the woman of fields and sheep,
flower to her chin, herds below,
the shepherdess of the *Idylls*.

Amaryllis is a print,
the plant roughly done, three faces
as its flower. Its leaves convey ash,
poison, and armor, protective of their little freak
and immune to falling fire, desperately garnishing
the stalk, the hallucinatory wand.
And there on top are the crippled smiles,
three women locked up, joined at the neck,
no hands for their hair.

An Education

The third generation antelope went off to school
intoxicated with St. Augustine and wild rye.

Great swales capped green beneath the animals
led to the veneration of wild-chance rhythm.

Black-outs occurred as well during peak hours
and off-seasons known as toxic atmosphere.

Despite it all, there was periodic grazing
in magazine racks. Pink nibbles, stark white teeth.

Always late, loping through crowds, bagged books,
and sweet concessions, the learned ungulate arrived.

Serpentine jazz inspired black-stocking hoofers.
There were no wooden fences they could not leap.

On a Winter Morning

I go rhino hunting and hear clichéd jazz about jazz, as if the mention
of Coleman or Mingus will save it.

As if a ghazal were twenty gay couples in tuxes.

Clever and crafted, widely spaced halves of lines tell stories
left to right and top to bottom, though still like the woman
I loved and had to leave because everything divided, added, or done
was always point three three three.

Amputating my arms is not the same as clipping a bird's wings.

Those things that begin as mysteries and at the end you know were solved
when they began . . .

Curated by various editors, it's all nouns and open mouths when, in fact,
cobblestones and frogs want to whack and swallow each other.

And just how do italics remind you of talcum?

The voices are clarinet and viola after piano and flute. Silk gowns dance
while bubble wrap is flattened.

Thus it begins, *eine kleine*, naughty *nacht*.

She adds Turkey to her breasts. Andy likes evasions. The page refreshes
itself and you are gone.

Two Visionary Stories

Now what was lost is found.
Aren't we happy it wasn't rage
but love
that pumped the vein so full,
every extremity
so full of good posture,
as if

one must look good,
as if the correct amount
of attention is on oneself

so as to free the intellect,
a lighthouse
on a promontory
whose beam goes round and round
while darkness rises and falls,

a cellist reading lines horizontally
while the music is all-at-once.

*

Big man/little man goes to the store,
change in his pocket, wind in his hair.

He likes to walk into it, the wind, that is,
for the feeling of speed, the chill on his teeth.

Hates the store, takes it all out of him,
has to count, feel the pressure of that palm,

down with the quarter, up for the penny.

Stealing From Nonsense

What diddle-dee-dum-dee-dee on the wings of less
is more and the soft body of the GDP? The mast leans
as if it had a sail, as if there were wind, the federation
adrift in choice. Oily bird, don't ship it now.

New descending a staircase, pear of my eye, fig of No.
On the list of favorite things of the day: feeding hair
to squadrons of clay. The early days of synesthesia
epidemic yield *lickolodean* and a wart which rests

on an unfurled accordion. A steamy, winter
night train is like an invoice but is, in fact, fore-
closure. One-way zipper. It is all about
foreshortening or early retirement, some rhymes.

Degrees of Gray In Any Burg

All the time it took you to read it
across and down (left to right, you assume)
while all the words were there
existing at one time if you just looked
at the book. It took you too long! Meanwhile,
I was trying to figure out how to skip over
the picture that interrupted the words
right in the center, and how they made sense
from left to right even when I skipped over
the steeple, the frozen falling leaves
of mostly three colors rendered
off-white, pearl-gray, and charcoal
in the brilliant sky. Top to bottom
made sense too, despite a pregnant cloud
and eyelash rain beneath a simple set
of nouns and verbs, and manicured grounds
above a name, a being modified
by an adjective from its past. The sum
of the book was like that photograph
of earth from a spacecraft. Your glance
absorbed it all, but did you notice?

Seasonal

Sweet work in front of a mirror,
all the world behind in terror.
Neat work in thinnest shadow,
fall in the north, spring in the south.

Horses and jeeps, mired in snow,
balk or stall. Somewhere, a mouth
nurses open to create surprise,
clock in death a second time, lift

an eyelid. Harmless flirting eyes
summer in Puerto Rico, then shift.
Plan nothing, she thinks. Funereal
winter holds, an eye and window

frosted over. A blind sky's missile
landed here, a new season's show.

Puffball Acceptance

I receive this communication irresistibly, still more so
its contents as I cross the lawn to Dora
sitting on a garden-seat under a lilac. I connect
with one of the learned professions of boats;
a favorable wind blowing, the signals for sailing
at her life upon her: to curl her hair, make sorrow,
hope, or disappointment. My heart turns

when she shows it to me. It was a town on the Upper Rhine.
Glancing around, I make a suitable reply. I observe how she rises
as tarnished as the others. We grasp each other
by the hand again, fatigued, attended by a modest
little parlor-maid in blue. "No. no," cries Emily,
clasping her hands together. "It must be passionless air,
that it seemed as if nothing could disturb."

At The End Of A Street

We went for a stroll in the garden of information.
We went for a stroll in the garden of disinformation.
The oak tree dropped leaves, the oak tree dropped lies.
The oak tree leafed out in lies, the oak tree dropped truth.
Such a tree cannot live and lie at the same time, such a tree
cannot inform and misinform in the same life with the same lie.

Poopy did his thing behind the dying dogwood tree.
Poopy died as the dogwood stepped forth to hide death.
Millicent said the clear path was now hidden and ruined.
Millicent meant gravel is not grass, that acorns are not glass.
Two kinds of trees, two kinds of paths are the problems we faced:
gravel and grass may mix and cross, whereas two lying trees cannot.

Afternoon presented an art show and a flea market;
thus the afternoon revealed a craft fair and a yard sale.
Many people walked by, stopped, and walked on; many cars slowed.
Many cars sped off, driven by people who had walked on to find them.
Some people make such a show of art that we stop to itch and scratch.
Some people are craftily driven, running as they walk, speeding off to stop.

All worlds repeat themselves, as do certain words
in topical conversations, or forests of conical conifers
in tropical settings. Over and over, grasses wave and part
for those moving slowly or hastily to lie down. What do they tell
themselves or another? Possibly the same thing every time, yes or no
most likely included, love as noun or verb, and one or both departing.

Both Silence and Speech Transgress

Goods can be defined as final product
or as intermediate goods
used in producing other goods.

Thus the smile without a future,
or its short-lived erasure, when
this moment can be taken into others.

Call the waiter to intervene
or break the lull yourself, begin
to tell the story you'll both forget,

which is important, and is not.
Maybe it's the word-idea of "sunrise"
that makes it into every day.

Both silence and speech transgress
what customers take for themselves.
Like random words in a future letter,

the speechless moment asserts itself
in troubled silence when the check arrives,
forgotten music, forgotten food in every day,
memorable in every sunrise.

Demise

Tricia says, "Come see the absolutely
delicious harbinger exiting
from my mouth." "It's probably
from the pudding," says Mom,
"Come do your homework,
then you might go to the prom."
Daughter starts scribbling,
dark scowl across her brow,
slaughter in her mind. The bowl,
an ark, with a white prow
beached at her nostrils. Lost
lunch break. What sweet Louis
offers, she takes. With luck, that
bunch beneath the fire escape!

Mimic

– after Daniel Bosch's "Sonnet Nabokov"

Learn now a deep fold's graceful sine
        a mirror
of an apex now an almost crippling climb
        terror
as every wrinkle smooths. How the brain unfolds
        is a dome
and then a globe, how you can see it all
        center
of yourself and all or a synaptic ship
        that fires
bow to stern the distance you must go
        the water
not water but the space inside now outside
        time.

Upon Reading David Graham's "Upon Reading
John Ashbery's Twenty-Fourth Collection of Poems"

This guy's got it down, that slow-dance/fast-dance twitch
that's like people dancing without music which is used to sell
a pill for achy joints. The people dancing are not afflicted
by that exactly, but are like bumper cars at Coney or Scat Sage's
slo-mo repetition of freight train coupling, four hours of that
cinematically enlarged and accompanied by a single soprano
saxaphone, extreme upper register which is supposed, we think,
to mimic singing steel as you hear it around 3 a.m. from across
the river, practicing for disaster, highly reminiscent of Mrs. Gorley's
chalk across the blackboard, as well as the famous shower scream
that kept us dirty, gritty, and with an edge seeping from our collars,
which did not bring stares, just a sort of accidental moving away.

Digression can be the back teeth of a maw you didn't mean to kiss,
whereas it was—to draw this out—those shiny incisors of his verbs
eliciting comparison unto the dance, and what he wrote the about
about is the sequined-dressed partner treated like an adjective, like
there's only one noun in the world and we all know who that is.
Say it big but say it quiet. We loved the way opening Penguin editions
could get you lost in an elevator or make you put your foot out
and down hard when you'd run out of stairs. Words about the words
are like that but you can eat an ice cream cone and keep an ear out
for a kid's giveaway scream while you mull them over and hear
multiple clicks when kaleidoscope pieces fall together into an acid doily.

In Lieu of an Ars Poetica

I've cut the string. The kite levitates. It hangs right in there at two o'clock, its red vibrant against the blue sky.

The birch bends beneath it. We are all in the wind and my link with the kite is strong. I can't bear to look down. My body feels the gusts and I become very aware of my ribs. The kite is motionless but I sense its minute pulse, its love with the wind.

Sal, my neighbor, comes out in the late afternoon and feels the air around me. No strings, Sal. No fish line, no radio-control. The damned kite just hangs there.

Almost evening, the sky a cobalt blue and the red kite with a halo. Sal has binoculars and is examining the kite for ailerons.

Let Sal demonstrate wonder: I am as buoyant as the kite. There's the bodiless voice of my neighbor, and myself, an ethereal witness, totally satisfied, thankful I have no hands to caress the kite.

Sal says I have a martini in my hand. Thanks, Sal. I lift it without looking at it, feel a tingle at my lips, then with one hearty gulp toast the kite. The feeling is impossible, like an ice cube floating in air.

It is evening and only I can see the kite, that diamond shape where there are no stars. In the morning there are no stars, and no kite. But there is space for another.

Poems That Arrived Without a Briefcase

In the museum of very modern art
a guard shouts, "Don't touch that!"
then swooshes back into a cardboard
cut-out of himself unable to speak.

*

The gate works only in the writing of it
and will not open in real life where
people have a compulsion to touch.

*

A glint occurs only in special circumstances
when the observer is of a certain height
and carries himself a certain way when the sun
peeks out and strikes the pebble just so.

*

A leaf flies past. But the windows are up.
A maple leaf. You are traveling there.
But the windows are up. The red leaf
is in the passenger seat, traveling south.

How quickly you made it real.

*

We harbor thoughts as if they were boats
that know a language of flags. When they leave
all we have is their breeze and ragged edges of color.

Novel Scattered in a Quarry

There are the names
painted on sloping strata,
white tears sliding toward rainwater.

The beads have collected
where sky is the final pit.
There are the holes drilled for dynamite,
abandoned premonitions.

Now you see forest on the edge,
threatening to spill over, isometrics
that raise your head. Up there is a
rusted crane, and below,
a steel worm.

Gaze into the pond. It is full
of false endings, full of those names.
One is trying to meet its wavering mate,
a backwards cousin.
You are the third party.

You can't make them meet.
The parts like their distance
and there is already completion.
They make sense when you go away.

Elegy for the Oldest Son

"But this isn't a rebellion," the colonel said. "It's a poor dead musician."
– Gabriel Garcia Marquez, *No One Writes To The Colonel*

How stupid to startle the family
from the threshold of sleep, to shatter
one's own face in a window
with night behind it. The moment
has the heaviness of lacquer—
these wraiths in nightgowns and goosebumps,
and then her voice, low and solitary.

Why do shoes fit tightly
on these occasions? One is carried
to exhaustion on concrete, surprised
by the train whistle, the pungent ballast,
a coach brought to one
like a notch in roulette. Into the seat,

into a half-sleep, night left ajar
and the hard black cases
pressing into their thighs. Later, in the suit
of concerts and death,
he would pierce the first formal silence
and the other would follow, hearing

how she came to him with a gesture of grace
so like the dusting of her skirts; how the wet-nurse
became "mama," molding little mouths
to her breasts. Mama had a way with secrets,
a way to turn them into orange blossoms,
and the wet nurse would press them
into the leaves of her simple dreams,
injuring him in this double affection. Often,

88

they stare into the bell of the trumpet,
into a vortex of night and trains,
until one or the other
makes his reflection on its rim.

Piracy

*. . . a Canadian yacht soloist had his throat slit
and was left for dead . . .* - Peter Munro

What are the swells
but a long note with a pulse

a string thick as a redwood
with a wide vibrato

the yacht another note
more felt than heard, a slap

of intent we might hear if
we hear a prow in the air

mainsail full of wind, a wake
reaching every shore

but the soloist's throat is cut
and the lazy boat has only

the wind's direction, its song
stolen, its voice adrift.

The Infinite Pianos

When the wind finally stopped
I saw how high the grass had grown.

That didn't matter—it was the piano
that was different, better, and fit in
now between plain and sky.

Its colorless notes
loved that corridor. They stole
blue, green, or sometimes ochre
from distant southern hills.

When company came,
we lay in the grass
away from the house, the barn, and the sheds
where there was plenty of piano room,

and every note
in the middle octaves sounded.

Nights fell with a dampened piano,
dawns broke with endless runs.

There was no end to the octaves,
no end up or down, and side by side
infinite pianos dimpled the sky.

The Music Exit

It can't just get up and walk out
a spurned lover, or someone who swallows
hype and discovers five or ten minutes
into it that he or she has seen or heard
it all before in different clothes.

Maybe it's Beethoven and solemnity
three times over annually,
or having seen spit fly
out of trombones, or a red cough
into a handkerchief in row one.

Maybe it's flowers on the stage
strewn beneath an ugly baritone,
or a slice of white silk lining
flashing through the seam of a torn
armpit, or even the thunk thunk thunk
of a ballerina's hard blunt toes.

It could be the silence flaring
out from an eighth note rest,
bows mid-air, brass and woodwind's
held breath, percussionist's
sticks and mallets frozen, hands

on drumheads, all rattle killed
like not hearing anymore
the roller-coaster of notes, syn-
copation, triplets, stairs of notes,
chains of sixteenth notes on a sheet
of music with no connection
between sight and sound. Rest

from something: the inner, inner ear
wants the caress, the soothing,
but a hand that is awake
lifts a hand that is asleep, the dead
weight of it practicing for eternity.

Gladdy's Blues

Gladdy Chromatic comes in lugging rubric
of mendacious ecology, doing rancid,
Barstow Eskimo blues. With banshee quickstep
and definite armpit augur, Gladdy's street pluck

roams swanlike beside an atheist anchovy.
I tell her to lay off Columbus gin mash,
Christlike schizophrenia, rheumatic greenery,
and to quit riding that lean needle surrey.

But then she goes into a flex Fargo crimp
and frog leitmotiv of augmented Mozart,
on and on about her affair with Cutaneous
Abram's janitorial ontogeny.

He's vertical immigrant proficient--
reminds her of acrylic where Chomsky
Budapest meets congestive roughshod Emily.
It was, she says, an inaccessible inflammation.

Beneath amazon skyscrape, hairpin radar
catches them and writes out a chronicle ticket
in tubular Illinois. That's when the Viking
restaurateur pulls a pantry prank smooth

as veterinarian clockwork, his impeccable
wiggly furze doing a fragmentary
lease clank. Gladdy's motto derision
of his superior effluvium births

minimum haiku: "Eighty-do-Madonna-
beyond-Bleecker," yells the Viking.
Gladdy's culvert gunman is witty
appointee with incumbent drink.

Gladdy and gunman climb aboard
an anthropogenic Packard omnibus,
skeedaddling like a sinister patch.
"Vanquish nutrition," they yell.

Live Music

Jazz swirls around me from the radio
and every note dips into live music
like a body that dives into water
and embraces water to keep from rising.
The piano chords are smoky voices
and hands touching. If I close
my eyes like the bass player,
the fat strings thump like heartbeat,
then something riding far above that.
Clouds are below us, though cloud-damp
clings for a moment to the fine hairs
of your arms, then evaporates
or is lost to body heat.
                              But really,
if you just jump from the floor
beneath you and dive
into the floor and miss it,
you'll know what this is like.

*

How can the tenor sax
make such fine stitches
between "I love you" and "I want"?
And its runs . . . like angels
tripping over themselves, scales
interrupting scales, blue,
then violet, then red, the trumpet
melting ice from the windshield
and the piano rolling down the window
for home cooking as they all
play together.

*

What is it about the way
they drop out and the floor sinks
and one of them weaves out of air
that has vanished three or four notes
in a row that everyone knows,
as with snapping fingers, tapping feet,
heads bobbing yes and no, lost
in the whole of it, we yawn,
laugh, and stay
past the time we should have left?

*

After a break, they ease in
with liquid piano, but after sixteen bars
they double up, the three of them tight as skin.

I must turn away from those two kissing over there.
I want to look at you
but that would be an early give-away
of something that's already happened.

But I know what keeps them
from leaving their instruments
and jumping into the crowd to sing
"I can't love you as long as I want to"
because up there they can.

*

Again the sax is weaving
above the piano, bass, and drums
when the piano snags a bit of summer breeze
and turns it into a squall,

but backs off before rain falls.
If drops would fall on a drum,
that would be next. But just
a darned second, who's that
singing about your face? I can't see
the horizon in those eyes.
I feel the beat, I feel
the beat, I feel the gray street
running under me, trumpet man
doubling the tempo, giant tambourines
ringing in my pillow.

*

Encore

How fast can you say, "one-two,
one-two-three-four"?
Because that's where this is,
walking to some hotel that
is that way to say goodnight.

The ear's desire
for a certain voice pulls in
the trumpet with its mute on
and triplets stair-step up the melody
while the drummer sizzles
the cymbal with brushes
like a thousand wands.

Now the bass player is dropping beats
on purpose and the piano wanders
in the upper octaves, still trying
to say goodnight.

Sideman

likes shade, knows the shadow dance.
Sundown is, like, really easy.

Heart Beat

Yesterday, when I had more heartbeats left,
I trusted the computer and gave it my birthdate.
It did the math and told me I'd had more or less
two-and-a-quarter billion heartbeats since then,
allowing, I suppose, for those teenage moments
when the heart stops more often than it should.
And, if the math is right, it said I have
a lottery's worth of heartbeats left.

What to do with those riches? Count them
one by one, as if they were going into a bank?
Spend them, because they are like oil
and I must get from here to there before
they run out? Or perhaps invest them
in quick returns? Or, as in music,

go back to a skipped beat, but this time
step into the stream again and let
the drummer go, lay this line of melody
next to another, plunk those fingers down
on a given length of string. Whatever rhythm there is
will find the heart that wants to go along.

Behind the Beat

At some point, the dark-suited, spent musicians
repeat the last eight bars
for the audience that wants an echo
to take home. That woman
wants it for reasons she has not told
the man, who wants it
for reasons he has not told the woman.

There is another man
to be talked about,
somone nearly equatorial, in white
in the evening, with a splash
of red somewhere
in his tie or the band in his hat.

There is some fascination in that,
as he meets musicians
on their break outside on the walk.
We notice and then
resume the conversation
like the flurry of their hands.

Everything seems to be wiped clean
with continuing music.
The white-suited man with a tambourine
and the woman with maracas,
both out of place and behind the beat,
are what we weave into this talk
and take home to repeat.

Here & There

An Imperfect Place

You would not walk barefoot
on this grass dried to stubble.
Snowmelt has not been enough
to keep it green, nor the summer monsoons,
but water enough to waste topsoil
and let the cinders rise.

You would not have chosen that shade
of barn-red, the mud color mixed by a child
with too many tints, which is daubed
onto the trailer and its add-ons. The porch
is saved by not having walls, a roofed
bit of space that extends miles to the west.

The roof is corrugated tin
that has easily borne winter snows
and tuned the rain. Windows are boarded
with warped plywood, sprinkles of glass
below them, fresh splinters of wood
beneath a bent hasp and a scarred lock.

You might think you'd been shaking
this thing called a "house,"
trying to get in.

Fear Via Place

South by southeast, I suppose, where thickets grow
and tangles weave green until it's black.

Places blind with growth blinding me, where I walk
right through a face in the day's brightest hour,

where I miss by a mile the hand that grabs a tree.
And if there could be shadow, that hand would cover mine

before it let go. But south by southwest would do,
where thin leaves grow, or even in the lava caves

where the mineral drip adds little to itself
and you would not know the person next to you

unless you talked real close, recognized the breath
and knew the sun was burning everything outside.

False Horizon

Walk to the end of the street, the very end
where hubcaps and used tires are sold,

where weeds dry out with half-opened buds
on acres of unsold lots, where broken glass

is a scattered necklace and there is a bus stop
where the bus always stops and chugs and

drives away, then walk a little further
until the street appears to narrow

because of brand-new shops with clearance sales
and grand openings, all of which slow you down,

those imports that didn't make the center of town,
the mixed stream of anglo women and immigrants,

a two-way street with one-way traffic
from the direction in which you walk,

toward the center, that way again.

Cone of Uncertainty

The cone of uncertainty extends from the eye
to possible landfall: a tiny port in the fetid south
and eastward to another tiny port in the fetid south
which reminds me of a blue wheelbarrow
with one point on the circumference of its wheel
firmly planted where I last left it waiting
to be steered by the arc made by my arms
and my hands grasping the handles, but that
is no cone of uncertainty and somehow geometry
backwards since an arc would not steer an apex
just as possible catastrophes cannot maneuver
their cause though they be within sight of the eye.

Bunny Wars

Here comes Peter Cottontail about your dark
hand clouding my skin, about the tar your face
pushed into my eyes, its origin in pre-Christian
fertility lore. The Hare and peach pits contain
small, minute amounts of cyanide. However
the saver has Easter bunnies hopping around
two researchers thinking the quantity of peach pits
available for Easter Bunny in memory of all bunnies
we couldn't save. Wood shavings and peach pits
add visual interest to our site update at Sears
Portrait Studio, where kids at the Astor Place Kmart
are treated to an unusual sight: the Easter Bunny
getting cuffed by New York City cops, the pen lines
of hollowed peaches. During WWII, civilians
were asked to save peach pits for the war effort. *Why?*
is not available. Click here to be redirected to our Home.

Animal Husbandry

Stir the more wholesome hay
whose dusty perfume may produce shrimp.
The average hog: its sow staggers alertly.

The stallion combines happily, mares extend,
studs prepare below anything.
Any thigh lights the mare—

a rough flash of clover,
scents with the bull are in vain,
an odd perfume dumps the clover.

First Amphibian

Scaly relic, spewing water, gulping air
into lungs that surprise a tiny brain

a new surplus of oxygen, maybe a thought
that comes of sharpened vision, but does

the horizon waver, do clumsy walkers undulate
and what does it mount in fear of too much air

in love with what does not resist so much
drowning doubly in its awakening?

Update

- for Obododimma Oha

Sheep dip by the numbers,
Alabama to Texarkana in sleep.
Rest stops include a narrow view,
sign monkeys, censorship providers.
Wind blows in the same direction
Wednesday through Friday,
then a mood of migration
wafts in through the slats.
Nobody knows what's going on.

Shock Value

Words that wore hatchets
in the heady days of high poetics
awake festooned with incomplete days.

What shall I make of that?
asks a plump little sausage
with boundless sexual appetite.

then defers to a narrative leafing out:
so many elections apparently decided,
so much collateral damage.

Suppose it went like this:
The ball bounced through the window
and the happy dog went after it.

Then reveal: This is the fourth floor
and the Cockapoo is a white petal
beside a crimson bloom.

Hummingbird in Zero Gravity

To push against air but not against gravity
must be like endless caresses that lead only
to endless caresses. But would it even know

direction? Would it go insane flying always
toward an endless ceiling? Or would it dive
toward home, unerringly toward one planet?

A quick nightmare: that it is flying through
average rainfall into the death of gardens.
Love on the way: it finds that it can hover

before its own feathers, which are always there
like a familiar cloud. The astronauts release
a thousand blossoms and it becomes lost

in the globe of heaven, a fragrant universe
from which it chooses a single blossom
that flying cannot bring close enough.

Fountain

- for Harriet Green, sculptor

She wants sympathy for the bent spine
and the hollowed insides,
the desperation of nowhere to lay eggs
but in another dead space.
Today she made its baby

and wants to lay it in front
of the skull where the mother
laid her eggs in the eye sockets.
How else to display them?
Perhaps the skull is also the father.

The baby is already empty.
The sides of its hollow come together
at the end to form another channel.
Anything poured into this baby
will simply flow out again.

Mockingbird Bouts

*The highly variable singing of the northern mockingbird
(Mimus polyglottus) is distinguishable from that of other
sympatric mimids by its organization into bouts: the bird's
tendency to repeat an element several times before proceeding
to another.* - Nicholas S. Thompson et al.

1.

A monk, a monk
on the mountain
through the rain. Beneath
a white cloud, a flame
in the evergreens.

2.

A paper and rag man
floats a boat, waves a flag,
picks his teeth with a mast.

3.

See how that cloud tapers and curls
at the end. It has a belly, it has
a waist, so why not a tongue?

4.

A butterfly tattoo, the glint
of a ring in a navel, and young
white breasts focusing the sun.
Shadows of umbrellas rush toward her.

5.

Three ways of drowning:
the great wave, repetitions
of the wave, a father curled
around his lungs.

6.

You see through your eyes
and he sees through his – as obvious
as heads and tails, left thumb, right thumb.

7.

A slender hand in a dream
moves like a fish in waters
of desire which slip
through her fingers,
rise from her toes,
and wear her like a sheen.

8.

For a moment, every leaf
on a tree has a face
but then it is fall, then winter.

9.

A pink daisy the size of a saucer
is clipped to straight black hair.
Her profile descends library stairs
and is gone when they turn
on themselves and also disappear.

10.

Something about edges—of a page, a screen,
the curb, a cliff, but not a blade—
all together when one fails to meet a friend.

11.

The emerald was
a shard of thick, green glass,
the coin a washer, the bird a leaf
in the echo of her singing.

12.

An olive tree is centered in its shadow,
a lizard freezes on a cinderblock wall,
a woman in a wheelchair rolls into the sun.

13.

The little toes like dew claws now—
footprint of a four-toed human
coming down a mountain, second or third thought
still not of himself.

14.

Day moon started as paper
and for a moment was no different
from everything around it
before it became a hole in blue sky.

15.

Mother's gown is made of blue paper,
as are her slippers, but her hair
is suddenly white at the end of a hallway.

16.

Guards wake from dreams of rain
to ruffles and flourishes from boiling clouds,
rifles and canon in the crash of a band.

17.

A place named *Deadman's Crossing*
could be anywhere among these rocks and trees.

18.

At night, every night
in the middle of the night: sounds
the animals couldn't have made.

19.

Yellow glow, post with lampshade
next to the tracks, in front of a house,
window full of darkness.

20.

A yucca's white blossoms fall
impaled on the yucca's leaves.
A jacaranda's violet blooms
lie whole on the lawn, crushed on the walk.

21.

Hair brushes against hair,
storm comes but doesn't storm,
yet there's joy walking into it.

22.

Ruts in the grass,
lakeside trash,
meatsmoke rising,
steel drum with grill.

23.

At the daily opera, the baritone
emits cigars of funnel smoke
below a tenor's hefty toot. Soprano
sharpens high C and rides its rail.

24.

Gunmetal mountains against the dawn,
the mind an umbrella turned inside out.

25.

He looks every which way in the wild wind
that turns downside up every leaf on the trees
and picks up dust and scatters it as if it had
four hands the size of those naked hills.

No End of Summer

Months beyond its boundaries,
at least one before and two after,
new blossoms limp, then fruitless tomato.

Water in the air but not on the ground,
dead center in a ring of mountains
below a ring of clouds.

And the ads! Fall and school,
leaves of a color months away,
each day nosing for fall or north wind,

anything but the scent of self
close by, too long a lover
dressed in damp sheets.

Anemone of Desire

Anchored on a sandy mound, hundreds of pale, pencil-thin penises
undulate in the waters, imagining the fluid that surrounds them
is a mouth.

An Almost Love Poem

There's a time when love wants to come again, but finally
it doesn't, not totally anyway, just some part
you can hear like footsteps' echo. Though the hallway's empty,
almost-love reverberates. Possibly, you want to be fooled,
make giant strides out of eyes deep with spring just realized,
the no-joking hyacinths in your face, and of course the smile
that simply transfers to your face, or yours to hers,
or even a sudden, mutual blossoming
witnessed by someone you made up and walked
through a desert night, where the waxy, white trumpets
of Echinopsis opened in moonlight, two at once,
and closed differently at dawn.

Reliquary

- *La musique savante manquena notre désir.*
                              - Rimbaud

It is the green and the pale
needles of the cedar which blow

equally across soil
that also moves. They take

little time across my shoe,
little time across your shoe.

The earth heaves
and my hand finally

crosses yours, like the shadow of a blade
which leans from the sun's face

that burns only
at this angle one time

before time is fixed and useless
under all the burning wheels.

They turn us under,
turn us over.

We are surprised in this cold
oneness by the dawn, the earth

gripped by two hands and two hands
in the earth. Don't we love

this locked motion? That digs in,
repeats from the center outward?

Wedding Tent

Once I saw a wedding tent on the beach.
One of the flaps tied back with a big white bow
had come undone and flailed about in the wind.
It made me feel unwelcome, as if it would slap me
if I tried to enter. Still, there was something exotic
about this temporary house of ceremony:
its peaked roof, the sandy floor, the way it swayed
side to side in the wind and in rhythm with the waves.

It was hard to tell if it was waiting or done with,
but footprints inside were preserved while outside
a layer of sand skittered across sand without white horses
and princes astride them. What birds there were
stood anchored with beaks into the wind. I wondered
what commotion there might be out there
beneath the whitecaps, but that was momentary.
I knew there'd be a crab looking for a shell,
a little train of seaweed following it inside.

Times When

Vast, empty, and unkempt lots
existed between houses and on corners.
Stakes were pounded in, tents went up,
corrals and booths. Bleating,
naying and grunting in the night,
machinery oiled into distant rhythm.
Tanned strangers wandered the neighborhood,
a canvas covered truck sat in the alley.
Some women wore no underwear. One woman
drew a boy into her. Her jewelry jangled
and a viscous liquid spilled from her, some
onto the boy. It was as if
the leaves of the forest had been crushed,
as if his scalp had been turned inside-out.

Magnetic Express

The conveyance is empty when it begins after a station break
and also very quiet, except for seats that squeak with motion.

Great murals slide by eyeless windows and windowless eyes;
wide, deep vistas of a million lives open up without a shock.

All seats are adjustable, aisles are as sand is to water,
the music like time itself. Headrests dream attainable dreams.

When newspapers spread out like that, they are as wings,
or just one newspaper in a fly's eye, multiple and unread.

Announcements: all true. For how could Vinedale be anything
other than Vinedale, its distance constant despite the speed?

One stop, two stops, three stops, stops all along the way,
even the beginning and the end are stops along this way.

Best thought of as Magnetic Express that flutters fearlessly
around a single polarity, it moves a whole city into a nation.

Should disaster befall it with the grace of one falling body,
the anesthesia of mass and consensus will comfort it.

Nation As Null Set

The west is their frontier
and the east a frontier for the others. As they chew
up the continent, they pass each other, go right through
each other, and there's this tiny dinging sound of a ring
bouncing on tile, or a washer hitting cement, or a bullet casing
bouncing off rock, ding ding in the two wakes.
The situation makes it possible
to explicitly define the results of blind warring
on certain invisible people who would otherwise
not be definable. Sure, they grow flowers and raise pets
but when they attend a party alone there are
two empty rooms instead of one.
Each is the foundation for the other
via secret couplings in a place where neither lives
and where great sums of almost identical money
are exchanged. It would be against the common good
to hold it to the light. Only now do we see the wisdom
of the flowering of story, the histories of others.

The Headlong Future

The home of Judge Roy Bean,
the crypts at Querétaro,
the Concord meeting house,

they all breathe the same air,
that of a barely remembered rain
or the invisible cloud
after a scattered pile of leaves.

It is air
not used to exhalations,
but one that breathes into us
and breathes into us
a long slow intake of breath. *Now*

does not exist, nor *then*,
and we continue breathing in. *Take*
it says, and we do, until we topple
into the headlong future

that never was
but is with the next breath.

Poems for the Dog Star

The jade knife wakes and hums
on Lu Chou's ebony table.

Lu Chou, asleep,
hurries in an elevator

to meet the dream woman
who becomes flesh and is destroyed

by the Ch-in sun.
The jade knife, leaving its place
in the spectrum, relays

to Lu Chou's parting eyes a blue line
that pierces the window: Lu Chou

cast into the black world
whose shell is light.

*

A cicada impaled on a sparrow's beak
does its thousand rattles
to rival the calls of the fledglings who eat it.

The old man
thinks the cicada is inside
and the bird outside, both alive,
though the cicada is not where it should be.

This affects his day.

All day he turns his ear
to the beginning of any sound: the trowel
in his wife's hand at the garden,
the turning of the cock for water.

Can the sun
make such a sound,
warming the dry leaf into a dish?

It is the quiet
that concerns him now,
the quiet broken by his daughter,

who is even now
close enough to be heard
but must come nearer; who, with the mother,
stands just the other side
of his ear and stares

into the smoking hole
of the evening's first meteor.

*

He yearns for the night porch
and its droning silence,
where the large family
is safely contained and seems
an afterthought in the thin house.

He remembers blue stick-figures
completed by the movement
of males in heavy snow,
the night pushed out, the chrysalis
worked to brittleness, a body

breaking into night
even as the jerky figures
pulled snow over the world of Lu Chou.

*

The woman who is not here
inhales the scent of blossoms
that explode with the train's speed.
        From the space
between two coaches, she sees again
a configuration of lake, volcano,
and heavily flowered shore.
It is the image of each day
        and once again
she expects the interminable green,
the lianas and their variegated darkness. This time
        the flowers lash
at the tight little city, a knot
that contracts, then unravels,
revealing at its center a sad horse
that turns in fences of tin:
        one last night,
she thinks, and the train climbs,
slowing on the flank of a cone
that is the twin of another,
        and on the lake
she imagines a plume of smoke
from the locomotive. Fire joins fire
in the water, like the red pistil
of an enormous flower
        that dips into itself.

*

In Lu Chou's childhood, the executioner
would play with two small helmets,
tiny bowls, really, sewn from the hind
found on the mountain. In them,
the sky had been reduced
to twelve large stars.
The pomegranate
had more; none in the orange
whose empty rind lay beside him.

But when, in his forgetfulness,
he turned inside-out one spangled shell,
the seeds of light were as his charges,

halved, halved again,

faster than the axe, invisible
in the double hood of night.

Two of a Kind

Time of life

Here today, born tomorrow,
noon of my mother's morning, noon, and night.
I rummage in the mornings,
rid of yesterday, peering at night's skirt,
born while the family slept.

*

The latest advisory & breaking news

The present is gone in an instant.
Anal seepage is worse than whistle in the lungs.
Sudden wind through an open house slams shut
an interior door. At the end of the story,
the appearance of stars does not explain cut hay.
Here's some thread, you are the needle. Go ahead.

Walking Down and Backwards in Walnut Canyon

After the switchbacks, early in the easy slope
to the bottom, you can risk jumping
onto the terrace below, then backtrack
through transition growth, a mix of juniper,
pine, cactus and agave. The scent of wet limestone
wraps you in the great, shaded funnel
where you find yourself, under a shelf,
squatting next to the groove
cut by fast, tumbling water. Empty pools
are within hand's reach, and fish bones
if you scratch into the waterless shore.
Simply look across the canyon, at eye level,
and there's a dark shelter, with the wall
of uniform stones and its doorway: neighbors
across the water that isn't there. Now
you'll want to straighten up, move that branch
from the way you came. But don't, because
then it will be a path, and the wrong one
because it was all different then,
and that is all I'm going to tell you.

About the Author

James Cervantes is the author of six previous collections of poetry. He was editor of *Porch*, a print journal, *The Salt River Review*, an online magazine, and is currently editing poetry for *Sol*, out of San Miguel de Allende. Cervantes has been publishing poetry in print since 1969 and almost exclusively online since 1997. Once upon a time, he could truthfully claim to be a professional musician, a cellist, as a matter of fact.

The selected poems in Sleepwalker's Songs come from six previous collections: from Mr. Bondo's Unshared Life, Vida Loca Books, 2007, Temporary Meaning, Hamilton Stone Editions, 2006, Changing the Subject, in collaboration with Halvard Johnson, Red Hen Press, 2004, Live Music (chapbook) Pecan Grove Press, 2001, The Headlong Future, New Rivers Press, St. Paul, MN, 1990, and The Year Is Approaching Snow, W.D. Hoffstadt & Sons, Syracuse, NY, 1981.

www.ingramcontent.com/pod-product-compliance
Lightning Source LLC
LaVergne TN
LVHW011244080426
835509LV00005B/622